HATE CRIME

IN AMERICA

FROM PREJUDICE TO VIOLENCE

by Danielle Smith-Llera

Consultant:
Frank Pezzella, Associate Professor of Criminal Justice
John Jay College of Criminal Justice, New York

Informed! is published by Compass Point Books, an imprint of Capstone.
1710 Roe Crest Drive
North Mankato, Minnesota 56003
www.capstonepub.com

Library of Congress Cataloging-in-Publication Data

Names: Smith-Llera, Danielle, 1971- author.
Title: Hate crime in America : from prejudice to violence / Danielle Smith-Llera.
Description: North Mankato : Compass Point Books, 2020. | Series: Informed!
  | Includes bibliographical references and index. | Audience: Ages 11-12
  | Summary: "Hate crime in the United States is on the rise. The FBI has
  reported that hate crimes rose by 17 percent in 2017, increasing for the
  third straight year, and the trend continued into 2018 and 2019. The
  crimes are most commonly motivated by hatred related to race, ethnicity,
  or country of origin. Many crimes are also motivated by bias against
  sexual orientation or gender identity. Students will learn why hate
  crime is on the rise and how they can help combat it"—Provided by
  publisher.
Identifiers: LCCN 2019037653 (print) | LCCN 2019037654 (ebook) | ISBN
  9780756564094 (hardcover) | ISBN 9780756565596 (paperback) | ISBN
  9780756564100 (adobe pdf)
Subjects: LCSH: Hate crimes—United States—Juvenile literature. | Hate
  crimes—Law and legislation—United States—Juvenile literature. |
  United States—Race relations—Juvenile literature.
Classification: LCC HV6773.52 .S65 2020 (print) | LCC HV6773.52 (ebook) |
  DDC 364.150973--dc23
LC record available at https://lccn.loc.gov/2019037653
LC ebook record available at https://lccn.loc.gov/2019037654

Image Credits
Alamy: Guy Corbishley, 36, Jim West, 52; Associated Press: Juan Lozano, 30, Zach D. Roberts, 9;
Getty Images: Kevin Moloney, 31; Library of Congress: 13, 14, 20; Newscom: Polaris/Erin Scott,
8, Polaris/Jeremy Hogan, 56, Reuters/Cathal McNaughton, 25, Reuters/Jonathan Alcorn, 16,
Reuters/Kevin Lamarque, 17, 38, Reuters/Loren Elliott, 18, Reuters/Mohammad Khursheed, 28,
Reuters/Stringer, 22, TNS/Red Huber, 26, UPI/Kevin Dietsch, 35, UPI/Kevin Liles, 12, ZUMA
Press/Go Nakamura, 7, ZUMA Press/K.C. Alfred, 54, ZUMA Press/Michael Nigro, 5, ZUMA
Press/Planetpix, 46; Shutterstock: AVN Photo Lab, cover (background), Rena Schild, 43.
Design Elements: Shutterstock

Editorial Credits
Editor: Michelle Bisson; Designer: Brann Garvey; Media Researcher: Eric Gohl; Production
Specialist: Kathy McColley

Consultant Credits:
Frank Pezzella, Associate Professor of Criminal Justice, John Jay College of Criminal Justice, New
York

All internet sites appearing in back matter were available and accurate when this book was sent
to press.

Printed and bound in the USA.
PA99

TABLE OF CONTENTS

Chapter One

Hatred in Plain Sight

The driver was dimly visible inside the gray car that lunged toward the crowd in Charlottesville, Virginia. Sunlight flashed off the moving metal as tires screeched—then screams broke out. The bumper launched people into the air in a scatter of shoes, sunglasses, and water bottles. After the collision, as many as 19 people lay in the street bleeding, dazed, or unconscious. One person, 32-year-old Heather Heyer, died from her injuries.

This tragedy on August 12, 2017, was no accident. Witnesses saw the car reverse away from the crowd, lurch forward, and accelerate into the many people filling the narrow street. A prosecutor argued in the courtroom that the driver, 20-year-old James Fields, had acted in anger. How could a gathering of people he didn't know fill him with such rage?

Fields had driven from Ohio to Charlottesville with a single purpose. He planned to join hundreds of

The protest in Charlottesville, Virginia, turned deadly when a car accelerated into the crowd, injuring more than a dozen and killing 32-year-old Heather Heyer.

mostly young, white men in a protest. They wanted to halt the city government's plan to remove a statue of Civil War General Robert E. Lee from a public park. For many in Charlottesville, the Confederate leader was a painful reminder of a time when white people enslaved black people in the U.S. But Fields and the other white supremacists in Charlottesville admired Lee and the racist attitudes of the Confederacy. They believed that white people were superior to all other races, including Jewish people. They came to Charlottesville to make their views known.

Before committing his violent crime, Fields had marched through the city with protesters. They carried

Confederate flags, clubs, shields, pepper spray, even guns. They shouted racial slurs and chanted, "White lives matter!" and the Nazi slogan, "Jews will not replace us!" Meanwhile, Heather Heyer and many other counterprotesters filled Charlottesville streets to shout back, raising their voices against bias and hate.

Fact

Those who commit hate crimes can encourage others to commit their own. A third of deadly hate crimes motivated by white supremacist views were inspired by others like them. Killers may choose to commit hate crimes on the anniversary of another hate crime.

Free Speech

Until the protest turned violent, the marchers were breaking no laws by voicing their hatred. The First Amendment of the United States Constitution protects everyone's right to free speech. This means that even beliefs and opinions that offend others are legal—unless they threaten someone directly or lead to violence. Before the march began, police took up positions around the city and local hospitals prepared beds for anyone injured.

No one doubted that Fields had turned his car into a deadly weapon. Photographs of his attack on

More than Just a Statue

High school student Zyahna Bryant launched the movement to remove the Robert E. Lee statue from the Charlottesville park. In 2016, the teenager wrote a petition to the city council. "I am offended every time I pass it. I am reminded over and over again of the pain of my ancestors and all of the fighting that they had to go through for us to be where we are now."

Riot police stood in front of the statue of General Robert E. Lee during the Charlottesville protest.

One month before the deadly 2017 rally, Bryant helped honor the memory of John Henry James, a black man targeted for his race. He was murdered in Charlottesville nearly 120 years earlier. Bryant was part of a group that collected soil from the place where James was hanged from a tree. They traveled to the headquarters of the Equal Justice Initiative in Montgomery, Alabama, to deliver the container etched with James's name. It joins a collection in the Community Remembrance Project that includes soil recovered from hate crimes committed from Tennessee to Maryland. The collection "helps to make our history of racial injustice more visible . . . and expresses our generation's resolve to confront the continuing challenges that racial inequality creates."

The plan to remove the Robert E. Lee statue came to a halt after the rally. As of June 2019 the Lee statue still stands in its original location.

counterprotesters, some holding "Black Lives Matter" signs, shocked many in the nation. For his actions in Charlottesville, Fields was convicted in a Virginia state court of malicious wounding and first-degree murder. But his crimes fell into a special category. That category brought him to a federal courtroom in February 2019. There he was charged with hate crimes. Hate crimes are motivated by bias against a person's race, country of origin, religion, sexual orientation, gender identity, or disability. In July 2019, the judge imposed a life sentence plus 419 years based on the severity of his crimes.

Proving a crime is motivated by hate can be difficult. Prosecutors presented evidence of Fields's bias against the

During the Charlottesville protest, white supremacists staged a demonstration in favor of keeping Confederate monuments. They were met by a crowd of more than 1,000 counterprotesters, and kept separated by riot police.

people he attacked. Before he drove to Charlottesville, his mother advised him in a text message to be careful. "We're not the one[s] who have to be careful," he texted back. Attached to his message was a picture of Adolf Hitler.

Fields was not the only person tried in court for carrying out hate crimes in Charlottesville that day. A surveillance camera in a downtown parking garage captured a group of white protesters beating a black counterprotester to the ground with clubs. They argued that they were defending themselves. The video shows an attacker dressed in combat gear, complete with goggles. The bleeding victim is seen trying to crawl away. The attackers left him with broken bones, a deep head wound, and a spinal injury. Video of the crime helped the judge and jury decide that the man was targeted because of his race.

The Charlottesville rally showcased how hate can inspire violence. The Department of Justice (DOJ) estimates

DeAndre Harris, who was severely beaten by white supremacist protesters, was himself originally charged with misdemeanor assault. He was found not guilty.

that 250,000 hate crimes take place each year. That's about one every 90 minutes. These crimes range from vandalism, robbery, and hate mail to physical attacks and murder.

Hate crimes can happen in grocery stores, places of worship, restaurants, parking lots, train compartments, traffic, or anywhere else people go. They can happen to almost anyone. Skin color is one factor that motivates hate crimes. Being born in another country—or having relatives who were—is another. But even white people born in the U.S. are not always safe. Being gay or transgender can trigger hate crimes. Having disabilities can too. And people who defend those targeted by hate crimes can become targets themselves. What's more, shock affects whole communites where hate crimes occur. "We all have a stake in building societies that are intolerant of intolerance," said Jonathan Greenblatt, director of the Anti-Defamation League.

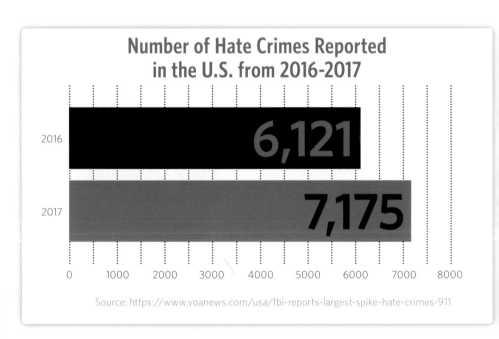

Number of Hate Crimes Reported in the U.S. from 2016-2017

Year	Number
2016	6,121
2017	7,175

Source: https://www.voanews.com/usa/fbi-reports-largest-spike-hate-crimes-911

Chapter Two

The Path of **Hate**

Video cameras captured 21-year-old Dylann Roof entering Emanuel African Methodist Episcopal Church in Charleston, South Carolina, in June 2015. Soon, desperate 911 calls captured the gunfire and screams inside. Survivors later described Roof sitting down with members of the mostly black church for a bible study. Then he began shooting, murdering nine people. Roof chose the church because he knew he would find black people inside. In 2017, Roof was convicted of hate crimes in a federal courtroom. He was sentenced to the death penalty.

Roof did not have a history of committing crimes. For some young perpetrators, the hate crime is a first offense. So what motivates them to do it?

Fact

The term *hate crime* was not used until the 1980s. But some experts point out that hatred of a victim doesn't always involve discrimination. They prefer the term *crimes motivated by bias.*

Dylann Roof was captured the day after he killed nine people. He immediately confessed to the murders. In January 2017, he said, "I do not regret what I did."

Feeling Under Attack

Powerful emotions brought white supremacists to protest in Charlottesville. They want a nation where white people hold the greatest power and wealth. The diversity of people and lifestyles in the United States fills them with anger and fear. These emotions are not new.

Confederate Army veterans organized the oldest U.S.-based white supremacist hate group, the Ku Klux Klan (KKK), in 1865. Since the Civil War ended slavery, KKK members have used fear and violence to intimidate people because of their race or religion.

From the end of the Civil War well into the 1920s and beyond, the Ku Klux Klan held public cross burnings attended by white people who cheered them on.

"White supremacy and racism didn't just arrive on August 11, 2017," said teen activist Zyahna Bryant. "It has always been here. It never really left."

History is full of examples of racism. Just a few miles from downtown Charlottesville, a white mob pulled a black man off a train in 1898. They accused him of a crime and the mob acted as judge, jury—and executioner. The mob killed the man by putting a noose around his neck and hanging him from a tree near the railroad tracks. This was a practice known as lynching. Over the decades, thousands of lynchings like this one have taken place across the country.

According to reports in 2017, people are targeted for their race or ethnicity in about 60 percent of hate crimes. Almost half of them are black. Other people targeted include Latinos, American Indians, and Asian Americans.

Marchers in Charlottesville wore swastikas to show their admiration for Adolf Hitler. The Nazi leader of Germany (1933-1945) organized the mass murder of about 6 million Jewish people in an attempted genocide during World War II. Jewish people have faced hate crimes in the U.S. too. In 1913 a Jewish man named Leo Frank, a resident of Atlanta, Georgia, was falsely accused of the murder of a young girl. A mob of white people tormented Jewish residents of the city, shouting for his execution. The mob then kidnapped him from prison and murdered him by hanging. In recent years, a person's religion has triggered more than 20 percent of hate crimes. More than half of those victims were Jewish. Muslims are the second most likely religious group to be targeted.

It is widely accepted that Leo Frank was falsely accused of murder—and then himself murdered by a mob—because he was Jewish. He was not linked to the crime by any evidence.

Today there are more than 1,000 hate groups in the U.S. The number has climbed steadily since 2000. That year the government released news that alarmed white supremacists, said Heidi Beirich. She publishes the Hatewatch blog of the Southern Poverty Law Center, a group that combats racism and promotes civil rights. The U.S. Census announced that white people would make up less than half the nation's population by the 2040s.

Through websites and message boards, hate groups spread fear that white people will soon be outnumbered. The target audience for their hate speech is generally young white men. Hate speech dehumanizes people and can make violence against them an easier choice.

Rejecting Hate

T.J. Leyden was only 14 years old when he joined a white supremacist group. He said it "gave me everything I lacked—identity, purpose, a direction in life. I felt a complete sense of right because I was preserving my identity and my culture." Fifteen years later he heard his three-year-old son use a racist slur and realized he didn't want him to grow up to be racist too. He got the courage to contact the Simon Wiesenthal Museum of Tolerance in Los Angeles. He met with a Jewish leader to apologize for his beliefs. He agreed to speak to audiences about giving up bias. He remembers "the greatest compassion I've ever experienced is when I spoke at a synagogue and a Jewish Holocaust survivor came up to me and said they forgave me."

The organization Life After Hate helps people leave hate groups. Often, members of these groups are afraid to leave. They fear becoming targets of hate crimes themselves. Leyden regularly receives death threats from hate groups.

On a website Roof maintained, he wrote about the day his views shifted to the extreme. He searched the internet for information about a suspected hate crime. In 2012 a white man shot an unarmed black teenager named Trayvon Martin in a Florida street. Roof's online search soon landed on white supremacist websites. There, propaganda claimed that black people were enemies and urged white people to defend themselves. Roof said he has "never been the same since that day."

When George Zimmerman shot Trayvon Martin, an unarmed teenager walking in an unfamiliar neighborhood, many immediately saw the action as a hate crime.

For Roof, hate speech was a powerful trigger for violence. "Well someone has to have the bravery to take it to the real world, and I guess that has to be me," he wrote. Roof's mother collapsed in a South Carolina courtroom from a heart attack after hearing how her son had planned the massacre. But he also earned admiration from like-minded extremists. A reporter heard someone at the Charlottesville rally shout, "Dylann Roof was a hero!"

Messages from government leaders can influence hate speech and hate crimes too.

After the election of President Trump, racism surged to a record high. KKK leader David Duke said that white supremacists voted for Trump "because he said he's going to take our country back." Popular TV and radio shows helped spread Trump's criticism of people of color, immigrants, and others to a wide audience—and it won him many voters, studies show.

Trump's response to the Charlottesville violence also sent a dangerous message about hate and violence. Instead of speaking out against Fields and his supporters, he said there were "some very fine people on both sides." It was a painful reminder that racism is still acceptable to some people in the nation. Many outraged people spoke out. "This is a time to lay blame . . . on white supremacists, on white nationalism, and on hatred," said Republican Senator Cory Gardner of Colorado. A 2018 poll found that 55 percent of voters said that, under Trump, people felt bolder about expressing racist views in public.

When President Trump spoke at a press conference about the events in Charlottesville, many were horrified when he equated those who protested white supremacy with those who advocated it.

An Invasion

White supremacists who voted for Donald Trump hoped he would help their cause. He promised to build a wall along the U.S.–Mexico border to keep immigrants out. Between 1990 and 2015, the number of immigrants living in the U.S. doubled. As of 2018, there were more than 44 million immigrants living in the U.S. Since the election, Latino families have been told to go back to their country, physically attacked, and murdered. Hate crimes in California alone increased by more than 50 percent between 2016 and 2018.

In August 2019, a 21-year-old white man wrote a vicious anti-immigrant manifesto online. Shortly after that, he opened fire in a Walmart shopping center in El Paso, Texas, a city on the U.S. border where many Hispanics live. At least 22 people died, and dozens were injured.

The crisis at the southern border of the United States has led to a rise in hate speech and hate crimes against brown and black people of color—citizens as well as migrants.

But discrimination against immigrants had already spiked after September 11, 2001. On that date, foreign terrorists flew hijacked airplanes into U.S. buildings, killing nearly 3,000 people. Anger quickly took over the nation. The terrorists were from Saudi Arabia.

Fact

The most well-known hate crimes are often the most rare. About 1 percent of hate crimes are committed by people who view bias as a mission. They often write long texts of racist ideas and carefully plan violent acts to express them.

To some people in the U.S., anyone who looked Arab or Muslim deserved to be punished. In the years since 9/11, people have set mosques on fire, thrown homemade bombs at their entrances, spray-painted graffitti on their doors, and even rammed into one with a pick-up truck. Hundreds of verbal and physical attacks against people of Middle Eastern backgrounds were reported in the days after 9/11—and have continued for years. And Trump's use of stereotypes and the support of media networks like Fox and Breitbart may have encouraged people to act on this bias. In 2017 Trump announced a ban on travelers from several, mostly Muslim, countries. Even though the ban was halted by the courts, Trump's attempt might have had an effect on his supporters. That year, the FBI reported that anti-Muslim hate crimes increased by 100 percent, the highest peak since 2001.

The terrorist attack against the United States on September 11, 2001, led to a rise in anti-Muslim hate crimes. After President Trump's election, such hate crimes soared again.

The Rising Number of Hate Groups in the U.S.

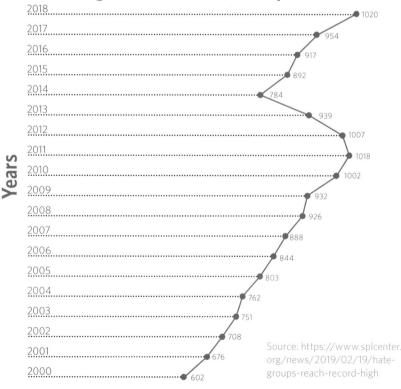

Years

Year	Number
2018	1020
2017	954
2016	917
2015	892
2014	784
2013	939
2012	1007
2011	1018
2010	1002
2009	932
2008	926
2007	888
2006	844
2005	803
2004	762
2003	751
2002	708
2001	676
2000	602

Source: https://www.splcenter.org/news/2019/02/19/hate-groups-reach-record-high

Hunting for Thrills

Just one month after Roof's crimes, a rowdy group carrying Confederate flags roamed Douglasville, Georgia. They were looking for black people to harass. The all-white group yelled racial slurs at guests at the outdoor birthday party of an eight-year-old black child. Pointing a gun at the adults and children, they threatened to shoot. Police arrived to form a barrier to protect the party guests from those threatening them. A Georgia judge ruled that the all-white group was guilty of crimes motivated by racism.

Hate crimes like these are far more common than those such as Roof's. They target people based on their biases, but at random, in public places such as streets or parks. So what causes people to commit these crimes? They may be looking for entertainment. They may also be looking for a sense of power over people. They may be using alcohol or drugs, which makes them more aggressive and less likely to consider the consequences of their actions. The white people in Georgia who terrorized black birthday party guests were sentenced to between six and 19 years in prison.

Fact

Between 1995 and 1996, 145 black churches were burned down on purpose. In 1996, President Bill Clinton signed the Church Arson Prevention Act, making it a federal crime to damage religious property or prevent people from practicing their religion. In the past 20 years, more than half of the fires in houses of worship were arson.

Chapter Three

A Broad **Impact**

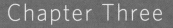

Charlottesville resident Jeanne Peterson needed a cane to limp into James Fields's trial in 2018. A year earlier, the tires of Fields's car had crushed her legs. Many surgeries were necessary to insert metal plates and screws into shattered bones. Another survivor explained to the court how Fields's car broke her pelvis and fractured her spine. She had nearly bled to death waiting for an ambulance.

James Fields was interviewed by a video link to his jail cell during his bail hearing.

Hate crimes can change survivors' lives forever. The majority of hate crimes involve violence, and 25 percent of attackers use a weapon. The injuries that result include bruises, broken teeth, stab wounds, bullet wounds, crushed skulls, and damage to internal organs. Medical bills can drain bank accounts and pile on debt. Injuries can also end careers when survivors are unable to attend school or go to work.

Current State of Hate Crime Laws

States with no hate crime laws

States with hate crime laws that aren't comprehensive

States (including D.C.) with comprehensive hate crime laws that cover: race, religion, ethnicity/ national origin, sexual orientation, gender, gender identity, and disability

Source: https://www.adl.org/50statesagainsthate

Invisible Injuries

A man on a train in Portland, Oregon, in 2017 lunged toward two teenage passengers shouting, "Muslims should die!" The teens were black and one was wearing a Muslim headscarf called a hijab. "It's like our faces were a trigger," Walia Mohamed, who was attacked, later said. The white attacker stabbed three passengers who stepped in to defend them, killing two and critically injuring a third. The two teenagers were not physically wounded. Yet hate crimes can do damage that lasts longer than many physical wounds. "Everywhere I go, I fear for my safety," Mohamed said.

Often physical injuries heal but trauma remains. One third of hate crimes take place near the homes of those attacked. This can shatter their sense of safety. Some people move away from their neighborhoods or cities after a hate crime. Others stay but feel haunted by the crime. Marissa Blair still wipes away tears when she walks along the street where her friend, Heather Heyer, was killed.

Marcus Martin's foot was crushed by Fields's car. Surgery has repaired his bones and ligaments but the sound of screeching tires still makes him panic. "When I see someone with a Confederate flag or with Confederate flag attire on, I don't take my eyes off of them. I just stare at them," Martin said. He often feels on edge, ready for another racist attack.

Physical therapists help hate crime survivors learn to use their bodies again after serious injuries. Psychologists and mental health counselors help them handle their emotions. Even with this help, fear, anger, and sadness can make their lives challenging for years.

Targeting a Community

A gunman walked into Jewish services inside the Tree of Life synagogue in Pittsburgh, Pennsylvania, in 2018. Robert Bowers shot 11 people. Survivors hiding in storage closets heard the gunshots that killed others in the congregation. The tragedy shook the entire city. That evening, grief and shock drew hundreds of people to gather at a Christian church less than a mile from the targeted synagogue. The ceremony for those murdered was moved outside to make space for the growing crowd. Meanwhile, fear spread across Jewish communities. They wondered if they were safe in their synagogues. They worried that wearing a yarmulke—a small cap that is a sign of religious observance—would trigger more hate and violence.

The community of Pittsburgh came together to commemorate those killed in the Tree of Life synagogue.

Another city was shaken when a man armed with a gun walked into a popular gay dance club in Orlando, Florida, in 2016. In one of the deadliest shootings in U.S. history, the attacker killed 49 people. Organizations immediately set up hotlines and walk-in clinics for people grieving the tragedy. "Anyone who needs help, we're here," one organization leader said.

The mass shooting at the Pulse nightclub was one of the most horrific in U.S. history.

Hate crimes do not have to result in death or injury to threaten people's sense of safety. The owner of a Muslim clothing store in Anaheim, California, reported a disturbing discovery to police in 2015. A Quran—the most important book in Muslim faith—shot full of bullet holes was left at his front door.

Centers and churches that welcome LGBTQ members are increasingly targeted for hate crimes. Rising acceptance of LGBTQ community members and the legalization of same-sex marriages has caused a rise in bias crimes against them. A brick was thrown through a stained-glass window of the First Unitarian Church in New Orleans in 2017. A public discussion on violence against the transgender community had just taken place. That same year, LGBTQ community centers across the nation had doors smashed in, graffitti sprayed on the walls, and at least one drive-by shooting. "It's a message that we shouldn't be in public, that we should be hidden away, that we should hide our identities," explained Sue Yacka, communications director of New York's Anti-Violence Project.

Gender Under Attack

People began following the life of transgender teen Jazz Jennings in 2015 on the TV show *I Am Jazz*. She feels lucky to have fans and supportive parents. "My story is one of happiness—one where a child was able to transition, able to be their true, authentic self," Jennings said. Yet she has experienced the cruelty transgender people face on the internet. Comments about her online have ranged from hurtful remarks to death threats. In 2017, more transgender people died from violence than in any previous year. Schools have found hateful graffiti and death threats inside bathrooms transgender students might use.

The government should do more to combat bias against transgender people, activists say. For example, the federal government should not restrict the freedom of transgender military service members to choose their gender.

As of 2019, 15 states did not have laws to protect against hate crimes due to sexual orientation or gender identity. But in 17 percent of hate crimes, someone's sexual orientation or gender identity was a trigger.

Bravely Facing Hate

Communities respond in many ways to the shock, anger, and fear of a hate crime. Survivors of hate crimes and their communities try to defend themselves from future attacks. Armed guards or police help keep watch over places where people who face bias gather. But armed guards or police posted at community centers, churches, synagogues, mosques, and temples can make them feel less safe.

Communities also work to stay connected in the aftermath of hate crimes. Just one day after the church shooting, The mayor of Charleston, Joe Riley, said that Roof had "this crazy idea that he would divide us. All this did was make us more united and love each other even more." When a man in Victoria, Texas, burned down a mosque in 2017, the Jewish community gave Muslim worshipers keys to their synagogue to use for their services.

Hate crimes reflect the worst of humanity, but they also reflect the best. When this mosque in Victoria, Texas, was burned in a hate crime, the Jewish and Muslim community came together. The Muslim and Jewish communities also came together when the Tree of Life synagogue was attacked.

Communities gather to comfort and support each other after a hate crime. After Orlando, LGBTQ community members and their supporters turned to social media. They added "We Are Orlando" and the rainbow flag, a symbol of the pride and diversity of the LGBTQ community, to their profile images. Mourners travel to place messages, flowers, and candles at the sites of hate crimes. Outside the Pittsburgh synagogue, people gathered to weep at 11 wooden Jewish stars, each bearing the name of someone who had been murdered inside. A gathering of people mourned the tragedy in Orlando by releasing rainbow-colored balloons into the sky.

Hard work awaits in the weeks, months, and years after a hate crime. Hate crimes force people to understand that bias exists in their community and in their country. Michael Coleman, a black resident of Charlottesville, remembers standing in a crowd of thousands holding candles and singing after the 2017 rally. Yet a year later he said little had changed. "As a community I honestly feel more divided than ever, which is sad," Coleman said.

But Nikuyah Walker, the city's first female black mayor, elected in January 2018, is hopeful. She believes that the rally has led to discussion that might help mend the relationship between black and white residents. Walker is patient. Charlottesville's history, she said, "is a white supremacist history, and it will take a long time to recover from that."

Demands for Justice

Community members also turn to governments to handle the aftermath of hate crimes. Two murders in 1998 stunned the nation with their cruelty. As a result, they would change the way the government handles hate crimes today.

In June of that year, three white men in Jasper, Texas, beat a black man. They chained James Byrd Jr. to the back of a car by his ankles and dragged him more than three miles that way.

"I can't see a human being doing this to another if you have any amount of humanity in you," said Louvon Harris, one of Byrd's sisters.

Mylinda Byrd Washington (left), 66, and Louvon Byrd Harris, 61, hold up photographs of their brother, James Byrd Jr., who had been viciously beaten and murdered 21 years earlier.

"They killed him because he was black," Sheriff Billy Rowles said. "This was the first time I heard the words 'hate crime'."

Byrd's torture and lynching brought top civil rights leaders and California Congresswoman Maxine Waters rushing to Jasper to demand justice. Two of Byrd's killers received the death penalty and one a life sentence.

In October 1998, a cyclist on a road in Laramie, Wyoming, thought he saw a scarecrow tied to a wooden fence. But it was 21-year-old Matthew Shepard. Shepard was openly gay. Two men had savagely beaten him into a coma. His mother could hardly recognize him in the hospital through stitches and bandages. Shepard died a few days later of his injuries. Many accused his killers of bias. President Bill Clinton spoke to the horrified nation and said the perpetrators were "full of hatred or full of fear or both."

Memorials to Matthew Shepard were left on the side of the highway where he was attacked because he was gay.

At the time of these murders, there was no law dealing with hate crimes in Texas, Wyoming, South Carolina, Georgia, or Arkansas.

Waiting for Justice

Until the mid-1900s, state governments handled hate groups on their own. Some states made wearing a mask in public illegal because the KKK used hoods to remain anonymous while committing crimes. But the laws did not stop hate groups from committing terrifying hate crimes. One of the most notorious was the 1963 bombing of a black church in Birmingham, Alabama, by three KKK members. That Sunday morning blast killed four young girls.

The federal government has investigated what came to be known as hate crimes since World War I. However, it was the job of state governments to pass their own hate crime laws. Then the 1964 murder of two white men and one black man traveling together in Mississippi helped change that. James Chaney, Andrew Goodman, and Michael Schwerner had volunteered to help black residents register to vote. When KKK members shot and buried them, the federal government sent hundreds of FBI agents to the state. But the state didn't convict the men of murder. It was left to the federal government to make sure that justice was done for the three victims, killed because of racism.

Congress passed the first federal hate crime law, but the Civil Rights Act of 1968 offered weak protection. It punished people who harrassed or hurt others because of their race, religion, or national origin. But the law did not include other groups. Also, the law only protected people while they were voting, attending public activities, or participating in any other activity protected by federal laws—not shopping or eating at a restaurant, for example.

The federal government did not move quickly to offer more thorough protection. Some people believe hate crime laws unfairly give harsher punishments, such as the death penalty, to those who commit hate crimes. But others argue that hate crimes are different from other crimes and deserve different punishments. For example, breaking down a home's door in a robbery is a crime. But it is a different crime when a perpetrator chooses a victim based on skin color, religion, ethnicity, gender, sexual orientation, or disability. The Supreme Court agreed when it ruled in 1993 that harsher punishments for hate crimes do not violate the Constitution.

Supporters also argue that federal hate crime laws are necessary because states do not protect all groups of people who face hate crimes. Though 46 states have passed hate crime laws, many do not include bias against people who are disabled, gay, or transgender. As of 2019, four states have not passed any hate crime laws. They include the states where Byrd and Shepard were murdered: Wyoming and Texas.

Chapter Four

Under **Protection**

Shepard's parents and Byrd's relatives were at the White House on October 28, 2009. TV showed President Obama signing a new law: the Matthew Shepard and James Byrd Jr. Hate Crimes Prevention Act (HCPA). Obama explained that the HCPA would "strengthen the protections against crimes based on the color of your skin, the faith in your heart, or the place of your birth." For the first time, a federal law would also protect people targeted for their sexual orientation or gender identity. The audience clapped and wiped away tears. After all, it had been 11 years since the murders of Byrd and Shepard.

Under the HCPA, more people who face discrimination gained protection. This group also includes people with disabilities. People with a physical, intellectual, or mental disability are at least 2.5 times more likely to be targets of violence than people without one. Hate crimes against the disabled have ranged from pushing people out of wheelchairs to torture and murder.

Two of James Byrd Jr.'s sisters, Louvon (center) and Betty (right), and President Barack Obama applauded one another when the hate crime prevention act named for both their brother and Matthew Shepard became law in 2009.

Fact

President Obama explained the reasons he signed the HCPA. "We must stand against crimes that are meant not only to break bones, but to break spirits—not only to inflict harm, but to instill fear ... the rights afforded every citizen under our Constitution mean nothing if we do not protect those rights—both from unjust laws and violent acts."

How HCPA Works

Federal judges and attorneys can review any crime in the nation where bias might play a role. In 2017, a South Carolina state court found Dylann Roof guilty of murder and sentenced him to life in prison. A federal court sentenced Roof to death for murders that were hate crimes.

The Department of Justice has charged more than 200 people with hate crimes since the HCPA was passed. Most of these crimes do not make national headlines but are serious. For example, a white man admitted to burning a large wooden cross in a black neighborhood in 2017, a centuries-old KKK tactic to scare residents.

Proving Hate in a Crime

A brutal crime took place in an apartment complex in Chapel Hill, North Carolina, in 2015. A resident barged into an apartment and shot three family members inside. Police investigated and decided that the murders were motivated by an argument over parking spaces. Other neighbors said that the killer had been threatening to all the residents. But many believed the family was targeted because they were Muslim and wore hijabs. The shooter had posted angry criticism of all religions online.

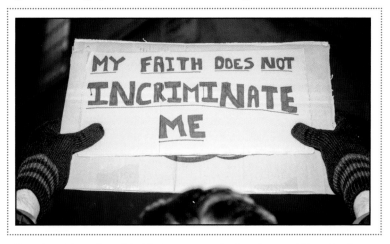

People gathered worldwide to express their outrage at the attack on a Muslim family in Chapel Hill, North Carolina.

Proving a hate crime is a challenge for any lawyer. First, the prosecutor must prove the defendant committed the crime. Then the prosecutor must prove why the defendant committed the crime. "TV usually depicts killers as cold and calculating," said law professor Joseph E. Kennedy, "but the mind of a murderer is often a chaotic, rage-filled mess."

Fact

Lawyers who participate in the "Stop Hate Project" take the cases of victims of suspected hate crimes in court for free. When Taylor Dumpson was elected the first female black student body president of American University in Washington, D.C., in 2017, a man used his white supremacist website to launch an online campaign to viciously harass Dumpson. Dumpson and the "Stop Hate Project" lawyers sued him for it.

Written and spoken words can provide evidence of a defendant's bias. Survivors often report hearing the defendant use hate speech during a crime. But there are other ways to express bias. Tattoos might display racist slogans and symbols. Investigators often discover that people who plan their hate crimes leave a trail of hate speech online. Before Bowers entered the Tree of Life synagogue, he had posted comments and memes on white supremacist websites that hinted at his plan. Others, like Roof, used websites and message boards to post manifestos of their white supremacist beliefs.

On the other hand, the motives of the shooter in the Orlando dance club are not entirely clear. The shooter called 911 during the massacre to announce that he was connected to a terrorist group based in the Middle East. Yet investigators discovered information that showed he was moved by anti-gay bias. He had spent two weeks visiting dance clubs, possibly to choose a place for the shooting.

All were popular meeting places for gay people. Police killed him as he carried out the massacre. The debate over whether he committed a hate crime or an act of terrorism continues.

As hate crimes spread, those who mourn strive to focus on the lives of those who were murdered rather than on the criminals who spew their hate.

Hate crimes are so difficult to prove that most people are found not guilty of this special kind of crime. As mentioned, the Department of Justice has charged more than 200 people with hate crimes since the HCPA passed. As of 2018, just 64 of those charges led to convictions.

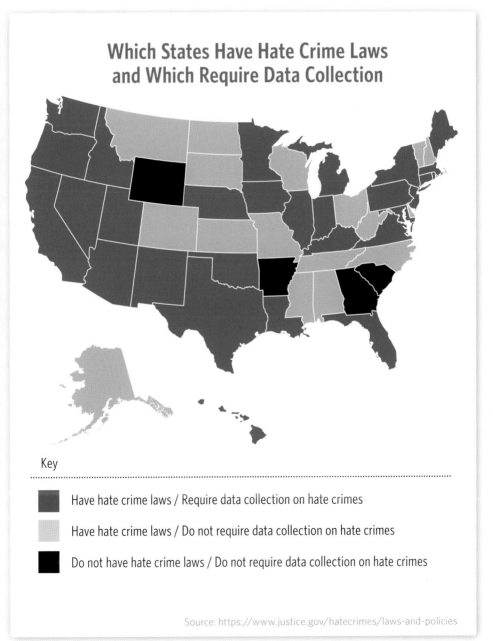

Which States Have Hate Crime Laws and Which Require Data Collection

Key

████ Have hate crime laws / Require data collection on hate crimes

░░░░ Have hate crime laws / Do not require data collection on hate crimes

████ Do not have hate crime laws / Do not require data collection on hate crimes

Source: https://www.justice.gov/hatecrimes/laws-and-policies

Chapter Five

Alarming News

The FBI has collected information on hate crimes since 1992. It tracks how many have happened and the characteristics of the people targeted. The FBI publishes these statistics every year. Since 2015, the reports show the number of hate crimes rising. In 2018, U.S. law enforcement agencies reported 17 percent more reported hate crimes than in 2017—the greatest jump since immediately after 9/11. Crimes against women, black people, Jewish people, and people with disabilities increased the most.

Fact

People with bias toward a particular group may not know that it contains diversity. For example, Hispanics or Latinos can be from Cuba, Mexico, Puerto Rico, South or Central America, and other countries with unique history and traditions. Hispanics can also be of any race.

Many experts believe the number of hate crimes is rising because the FBI is receiving more accurate information from survivors, police, and leaders of state governments. "Without accurate reporting we don't have a real sense of how widespread hate crimes are and what needs to be done to address bias in society," Anti-Defamation League director Jonathan Greenblatt has said. But many challenges stand in the way of collecting this crucial information.

Dangerous Games

Decades ago, hate groups attracted new members by passing out pamphlets or meeting possible converts face-to-face. Today, multiplayer video games allow hate group members to meet and even befriend young people. Through chat rooms and livestreams, white supremacists share links to propaganda websites. One father in Colorado was devastated to find white supremacist propaganda that his 15-year-old son had printed from the home computer. "I was crying. I felt like a failure that a child that I had raised would be remotely interested in that sort of stuff," he said.

Though this problem does not happen often, experts fear the situation could get worse. The FBI cannot monitor hundreds of millions of users chatting and texting. Investigating an incident is also difficult because hate group members often use fake names. Video game companies mostly depend on users to report offensive material.

Fear Stands in the Way

More than 50 percent of people who believe they have experienced a hate crime may not report the incident to police. They fear revenge from attackers or their supporters. A week after Matthew Shepard died, anti-gay protesters gathered outside the Wyoming church where his service was taking place. They harassed those attending with anti-gay hate speech. Police stood by with bomb-sniffing dogs. Shepard's family members wore bulletproof vests. Even after death, a person can be targeted for revenge. James Byrd Jr.'s grave in Jasper, Texas, was protected by a tall metal fence for years because it had been vandalized. The town did not remove the fence until April 2019. Shepard's family kept his ashes for 20 years. In 2018, they were invited to bury them in the safety of the Washington National Cathedral in the nation's capital.

Fear prevents survivors of hate crimes from turning to police for help. They may think police are biased against them. Indeed, studies have found that, in some parts of the U.S., police are twice as likely to search the cars of black and Hispanic drivers than of white drivers. Some police departments have been overly forceful when handling non-white suspects. When a community feels mistreated by police, mistrust grows.

Immigrants may avoid the police after a hate crime. They worry that going to the police could lead to deportation—especially since the election of President Trump. More than half of the police officers in one study said that this fear prevents them from keeping immigrants safe from hate crimes. When those who commit hate crimes go unpunished, hate crimes can rise in those communities. Everyone's safety depends on the investigation of hate crimes.

In 2017, thousands rallied in Washington, D.C., and around the nation to protest President Trump's proposed travel ban.

Police Reporting

The FBI collects data for its yearly hate crime reports in two ways. It collects information from police departments, and from individuals across the U.S. Still, it is difficult to know exactly how many hate crimes take place each year.

The FBI collects information from about 160,000 people across the nation. These people are randomly selected to participate in interviews. They complete a questionnaire called the National Crime Victimization Survey (NCVS). But many issues can lead to inaccurate results even when gathering information from survivors themselves. What if people report a crime without saying that it could have been motivated by bias? What if they don't trust that reporting a hate crime on a government form will actually help them?

Collecting accurate hate crime data from police departments can be challenging too. Police departments share hate crime data with the FBI through a program called Uniform Crime Reporting (UCR). Participation is voluntary. So there are no penalties for departments that do not participate. Out of 16,000 law enforcement agencies, just 2,000 reported hate crimes in 2017.

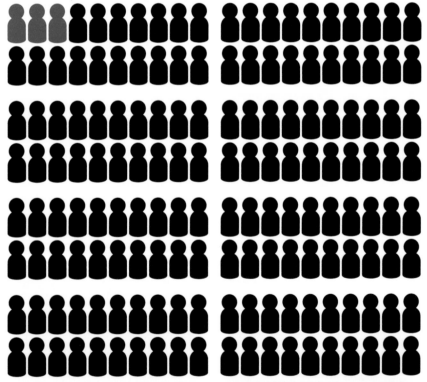

Hate Crimes Reporting Gap

In 2015, the National Crime Victimization Survey conducted by the Bureau of Justice Statistics estimated that 207,880 hate crimes occurred in the U.S. In the same year, the FBI's Uniform Crime Reporting Hate Crime Statistics show that only 5,850 were reported by local law enforcement agencies.

Hate Crimes Reported

Hate Crimes Occurred

Source: https://www.niot.org/stop-hate-action-kits/law-enforcement-response-hate

The data from police departments that do participate in the UCR are not always accurate either. Only 12 states have laws requiring police training in how to identify and investigate hate crimes. Mistakes also happen when a crime is not recorded as a hate crime. For example, Miami, Florida, with a population of half a million people, reported no hate crimes in 2017. Las Vegas, Nevada, didn't report any either until a city official corrected its data to report that 61 hate crimes had actually taken place.

Hate crime experts are concerned about the enormous difference between results from these two methods. U.S. households have reported about 250,000 hate crimes each year. Meanwhile, UCR data show that about 7,000 hate crimes take place yearly. The size of the hate crime problem is greatly misunderstood.

What Leaders Say Matters

Some experts believe that hate crimes are on the rise. They have analyzed data from cities and states across the nation. From this, they've concluded that government leaders can influence hate crime numbers. The election of the nation's first black president, Barack Obama, upset white supremacists. The number of hate crimes and hate groups spiked when he was first elected, though it went down again during his second term.

Government leaders send messages about bias in many ways. The South Carolina state house still displayed a Confederate flag when Dylann Roof decided to murder black people. Symbols can send the message that bias is acceptable. Nikki Haley, then South Carolina's governor, had the Confederate flag removed less than a month after Roof massacred the people inside the Emanuel African Methodist Episcopal Church.

Nikki Haley, then governor of South Carolina, was embraced by Reverend Norvel Goff following the ceremony taking down the Confederate flag from the State House.

Government leaders' words are powerful too. In 2018, a white candidate for U.S. Senate, Cindy Hyde-Smith, was running against a black opponent, Mike Espy. She made a joke about attending a "public hanging." Even supporters in her own political party were disgusted. Businesses that had donated to her campaign wanted their money back. On the night before the election, someone hung rope nooses from a tree at the Mississippi State Capitol. Handwritten signs placed nearby protested hate crimes in Mississippi—the state that for almost 90 years held the record for the most in the nation. But despite her comments, Hyde-Smith won the election.

Donald Trump has demonstrated how a president can influence hate crimes. He has made insulting public comments about Latinos, Muslims, women, disabled people, and other groups. He describes immigrants as dangerous and believes a fortresslike wall along the border with Mexico and a ban on Muslim travelers will make the United States safer.

Trump's ideas are exciting to people who resent the nation's diversity. In 2016, hundreds of hate group members at a gathering in Washington, D.C., celebrated his election victory with cheers and arms lifted in Nazi salutes. From the podium, one hate group leader shouted a phrase similar to one used by Hitler's supporters, "Hail Trump, hail our people, hail victory!" In the first 10 days after the election, the Southern Poverty Law Center counted almost 900 events where people of color faced hate in some way. Across the nation, vicious racist hate speech appeared in chalk, pen, and spray paint inside and outside of public buildings. Some schools noticed a spike in hate speech in their hallways on the day after the election.

School Troubles

More than 10 percent of all hate crimes in 2017 took place in schools and universities. These crimes include swastikas and racial slurs scratched into bathroom tiles. A Latina student found a note slipped into her backpack that said "Go back to Mexico." A fifth grade Muslim student received anonymous notes that said "You're a terrorist" and "I will kill you." A middle school student made a video with a rifle and threats to murder people of other races. Schools have set up hotlines for parents and students to report incidents motivated by bias.

School staff struggle with many questions. How do they punish students who commit or threaten to commit hate crimes without rewarding them with attention and encouraging other students to copy them? How can they respect students' freedom of speech without being too lenient on those who show bias or commit hate crimes? And most importantly, how can schools punish these biased students while also teaching them tolerance?

Researchers cannot confirm that Trump's words cause hate crimes. But they point out that his name and campaign slogan have been spoken and written by people committing hate crimes. One study found that hate crimes rose more than 225 percent in areas where Trump spoke publicly before the election. The number of hate groups increased by 30 percent between 2015 and 2019, a period that includes Trump's candidacy and term in office.

There is no doubt that Trump's words have caused fear among minority groups. Polls show that since his election, people fear hate crimes happening to them more than they did a decade ago. Many noticed that the El Paso shooter's manifesto calling his attack "a response to the Hispanic invasion of Texas" sounded like Trump's anti-immigration statements. Meanwhile, hate crimes against the LGBTQ community in Washington, D.C., have almost doubled. "We're seeing an unmistakable trend of increases," said Brian Levin, director of California's Center for Hate and Extremism. He says that hate crime data "shows that we're in a new era that started four or five years ago."

The attitudes and words of government leaders may even influence the way police handle hate crimes. When Trump calls immigrants "criminals" or "terrorists," police may take hate crimes against those groups less seriously. They may be less likely to identify or report a hate crime.

Trump's words in the aftermath of the deadly 2017 Charlottesville protest shocked many in the nation. He blamed "both sides"—that is, the protesters and the counterprotesters. Former President Obama criticized Trump's response and offered firm advice on how to deal with bias. "We are Americans. We're supposed to stand up to bullies. Not follow them," Obama said.

Chapter Six

Battling Bias

Matthew Shepard's parents asked lawyers not to push for the death penalty for his son's killers. Matthew Shepard's father, Dennis, spoke to Aaron McKinney in a Laramie, Wyoming, courtroom in 1999. "Mr. McKinney, I am going to grant you life, as hard as it is for me to do so, because of Matthew," he said. "Every time that you wake up in that prison cell, remember that you had the opportunity and the ability to stop your actions that night." The jury sentenced McKinney to life in prison instead of death. Russell Henderson was also charged with Shepard's murder and sentenced to life in prison.

Severe punishments send firm messages about the government's attitude toward hate crimes. Yet hate crimes still take place across the nation every day. "We wanted the system to fix things through punishment. We now believe punishment doesn't end violence—it perpetuates it," said Audacia Ray of the New York Anti-Violence Project. Beyond police stations and courthouses, people of all ages are trying to stop hate crimes *before* they happen.

A Group Effort

Groups targeted by hate crimes cooperate to fight bias together. Communities Against Hate is an organization formed by people who are Muslim, Jewish, Asian American, transgender, and who have disabilities, and by other groups that face discrimination. The group helps those who are afraid to report a hate crime they have experienced. The organization can find them lawyers, therapists, and other assistance. Their website urges survivors to call the hotline or email their story. "By sharing what you experienced or witnessed, you can educate the public, empower others. . . . And we come together to advocate for a better America."

One month after the Charlottesville protest in 2017, more than 80 organizations signed a letter to the Department of Justice in Washington, D.C. This group represented many of the nation's races, ethnicities, religions, genders, and sexual orientations. They included teachers, lawyers, religious leaders, and activists. This diverse group offered a single opinion: The government needs to use several strategies at once to combat hate crimes.

A Personal Approach

How can the federal government encourage police to identify and report hate crimes? Enthusiasm for the HCPA was high in 2009. Federal agents educated thousands of police officers in person and online about the new laws. They trained police to recognize a hate crime and to collect evidence to prove bias. One month after the Charlottesville rally, activists from 80 civil rights, religious, educational, and professional groups suggested that this intense police training be offered again. They also recommended rewarding police departments for doing the extra work that hate crime investigations require.

How can government leaders encourage hate crime survivors to call 911 when they are fearful? Some communities are already using a simple and powerful way to build their trust. Government leaders and police sit and talk face-to-face with community members to hear their concerns. This type of meeting is called a roundtable—a discussion where everyone speaks and listens to each other. Police know they can better protect hate crime survivors and their communities if they have a positive relationship. "They have to first see us as an equal, as a friend, as a partner. And that takes time," says Christopher Keeling, a hate crime unit detective in Los Angeles.

Learning Tolerance

Most people who commit hate crimes are white, male, and under age 20. By this time, they may already be influenced by bias. By the age of four, children notice the differences between races. By age 12, children may develop stereotypes about people of other races and groups. In middle school, students often choose to sit with others who share similarities such as race and gender.

Some schools are working to stop bias before it becomes a habit. Millions of children of all ages across the U.S. have participated in the annual "Mix It Up at Lunch Day." Each student sits next to someone he or she doesn't know. Teachers provide questions to help the students get to know each other.

The Waverly Middle School in Lansing, Michigan, is just one of many schools nationwide that participate in "Mix It Up at Lunch Day."

Schools also focus on an important reason for bias: fear of difference. Celebrations of other cultures introduce students to different languages, foods, music, and traditions. Classroom lessons that include a diverse group of historical figures also teach tolerance. For example, California and New Jersey require public schools to teach about important people in LGBTQ history and also about those with disabilities.

Students Teach Tolerance

After several hate incidents in 2017, a high school in Brookline, Massachusetts, turned to the Anti-Defamation League for help. Thirty students were selected for three days of training. They learned to hold their own workshops to teach tolerance in their own schools. "So if I affect ten kids, they affect one hundred kids who affect a thousand kids," explained a workshop participant. In one activity, students stood in a large circle holding strings to make a "web of unity." It illustrated how a diverse community can feel connected.

More than 4,000 students across the country have participated in this program, called "A World of Difference." These lessons have reached an estimated 300,000 students through student-led workshops.

As hate crime numbers rise, so have requests for this program.

Words as Weapons

Roof's crimes prove that hate speech can turn into hate crimes. For example, anti-Jewish violence rose by 37 percent in 2017. Online anti-Jewish hate speech spiked too. A 19-year-old man in San Diego, California, spent a year and a half reading about white supremacism online before he bought a weapon. In 2019 he attacked the Chabad of Poway synagogue in San Diego, California, opening fire and injuring three people, including the rabbi, and killing a female congregant who jumped in front of the rabbi to save his life. "We should not kid ourselves that online hate will stay online," says Anti-Defamation League vice president Adam Neufeld. "Even if a small percentage of those folks active online go on to commit a hate crime, it's something well beyond what we've seen for America."

Lori Gilbert-Kaye, a member of the Chabad of Poway synagogue, was killed when she jumped in front of the rabbi to protect him from a shooter. Her daughter, Hannah Kaye, spoke about her at a memorial service there.

A Hate Crime Happens When. . .

. . . someone is hostile to another person because of their disability, nationality, race, religion, sexual orientation, or transgender identity. They show their hostility by:

Intimidating	Harassing	Damaging Property	Acting Violently

Source: https://www.cps.gov.uk/hate-crime

Activists have pressured internet companies to ban users who post threatening hate speech on websites, message boards, public chats, and blogs. Internet companies are listening. Companies including Facebook, Google, and Twitter removed 28 percent of illegal hate speech in 2017. In 2019 they removed 72 percent of it.

Another Protest

For weeks in the summer of 2018, Washington, D.C., was on edge. White supremacists were planning a large protest in the nation's capital. Police prepared themselves. On August 12, 2018—exactly one year after the deadly Charlottesville protest—thousands of people gathered near the White House. But fewer than 30 of them were white supremacists. Most were protesting against them. Hate group leaders admitted that most of their supporters were afraid to come after the consequences of the Charlottesville protest. In the year since, a few had been arrested and were on trial for hate crimes. Many others were harassed on social media, fired from their jobs, and even rejected by family members for their biased views.

An anniversary rally in 2018 planned by those who had organized the Unite the Right protest in Charlottesville the previous year drew thousands more counterprotesters than white nationalist protesters.

Some counterprotesters held posters with photographs of those killed in hate crimes. Others held a long banner that read in large, colorful letters, "Unite Against Hate." The tiny group of white supremacists ended their march early and the vast crowd of counterprotesters cheered. The day ended with relief, but also disbelief. One sign read simply, "I can't believe I have to protest Nazis in 2018."

GET INVOLVED

Join your community members in cleaning up public areas that have been vandalized with words of hate. Volunteers cleaned off swastikas and offensive language spray-painted on a New York City playground, for example.

Pay close attention to language that makes other people seem inferior. Talking about undocumented immigrants simply as "illegals" is an example. Find the courage to tell a friend that jokes based on bias are not funny. Report online hate speech that bullies, harasses, or intimidates others.

Help people see that everyone is equal and worthy. Look out for bullying at school and stand up for those being targeted. Try to include new people in social groups so no one is excluded.

Plan a "Mix It Up at Lunch Day" at your school with the help of this website: https://www.tolerance.org/mix-it-up/getting-started

Talk to your teachers and principal about bringing Anti-Defamation League programs like "World of Difference" and "No Place for Hate" to your school to help teach tolerance: https://www.adl.org/who-we-are/our-organization/signature-programs/no-place-for-hate; https://www.adl.org/who-we-are/our-organization/signature-programs/a-world-of-difference-institute

Celebrate diversity by planning or participating in multicultural events at school.

GLOSSARY

activist—a person who works for social or political change

bias—to favor or disfavor someone or a group of people over others, usually in an unfair way

counterprotester—someone who opposes a protest

data—facts such as measurements or observations

defendant—someone accused of a crime

deport—to force someone to leave the country, especially if they have no legal right to be there

diversity—having many different elements, such as a classroom of students with many different backgrounds

genocide—the murder of a large group that shares a characteristic such as religion or ethnicity

harass—to bother in an aggressive way

LGBTQ—stands for lesbian/gay/bisexual/transgender/queer

lynch—to kill someone without a legal trial and usually by a mob of people

manifesto—written statement of beliefs and ideas

perpetrator—someone who causes harm on purpose

propaganda—information spread to try to influence people's thinking, often not completely true or fair

prosecutor—lawyer who tries to prove someone is guilty of a crime

statistics—a collection of facts that is analyzed

tolerance—accepting opinions, beliefs, and behavior that are different from one's own

trauma—an experience that leaves a person with physical or emotional damage (or both) that lasts a long time

vandalism—destruction of public or private property on purpose

yarmulke—a small cap worn by religious Jewish boys and men

ADDITIONAL RESOURCES

Critical Thinking Questions

Activists do not believe that punishments prevent hate crimes. Do you agree or disagree? Use what you have learned about why hate crimes happen to support your answer.

Why do police and activists say that hate crimes threaten everyone's safety? Do you think that anyone could become the target of bias and violence, no matter their race, religion, skin color, or any other characteristic? Why or why not?

Have you ever held a stereotype that influenced your attitude toward someone? If so, how did this attitude change after you got to know them?

Further Reading

Heitkamp, Kristina Lyn. *Confronting Anti-Semitism.* New York: Rosen Young Adult, 2018.

Krasner, Barbara. *Hate Crimes.* New York: Greenhaven Publishing, 2017.

Miller, Michael. *Exposing Hate: Prejudice, Hatred, and Violence in Action.* Minneapolis: Lerner Publishing Group, 2019.

Internet Sites

Kids' Health: What Is Diversity?
https://www.cyh.com/HealthTopics/HealthTopicDetailsKids.aspx?p=335&np=286&id=2345

Not in Our Town
https://www.niot.org/nios-video/leaving-positive-footprint

Stop Bullying
https://www.stopbullying.gov/kids/what-you-can-do/index.html

SOURCE NOTES

p. 6, "Jews will not replace…" David Neiwert, "When white nationalists chant their weird slogans, what do they mean?" Southern Poverty Law Center, October 10, 2017, https://www.splcenter.org/hatewatch/2017/10/10/when-white-nationalists-chant-their-weird-slogans-what-do-they-mean Accessed July 16, 2019.

p. 9, "We're not the one[s]…" Farah Stockman, "In Charlottesville Murder Trial, Courtroom Relives Trauma of a Violent Day," The New York Times, December 5, 2018, https://www.nytimes.com/2018/12/05/us/charlottesville-trial-fields.html Accessed July 16, 2019.

p. 10, "We all have a stake…" Jonathan A. Greenblatt and Elisa Massimino, "Global Crises Are Overshadowing Hate Crimes," Time, May 5, 2016, https://time.com/4318817/hate-crimes/ Accessed July 16, 2019.

p. 13, "White supremacy and…" Zyahna Bryant, "One Year Since Charlottesville, How the City Has Reckoned with Its White Supremacist, Racist History," Teen Vogue, August 7, 2018, https://www.teenvogue.com/story/one-year-since-charlottesville-op-ed-white-supremacist-racist-history Accessed July 16, 2019.

p. 16, "never been the same…." "Ten Ways to Fight Hate: A Community Response Guide," Southern Poverty Law Center, August 14, 2017, https://www.splcenter.org/20170814/ten-ways-fight-hate-community-response-guide Accessed July 17, 2019.

p. 16, "Well someone has to…" Frances Robles, "Dylann Roof Photos and a Manifesto Are Posted on Website," The New York Times, June 20, 2015, https://www.nytimes.com/2015/06/21/us/dylann-storm-roof-photos-website-charleston-church-shooting.html Accessed July 17, 2019.

p. 16, "Dylann Roof was…" Joe Heim, "Recounting a day of rage, hate, violence and death," The Washington Post, August 14, 2017, https://www.washingtonpost.com/graphics/2017/local/charlottesville-timeline/?noredirect=on&utm_term=.d5974b9b0aa6 Accessed July 17, 2019.

p. 17, "because he said…" Hilary Hanson, "Ex-KKK Leader David Duke Says White Supremacists Will 'Fulfill' Trump's Promises," Huffington Post, August 12, 2017, https://www.huffpost.com/entry/david-duke-charlottesville-rally-trump_n_598f3ca8e4b0909642974a10 Accessed July 17, 2019.

p. 17, "some very fine people…" Rose Gray, "Trump Defends White-Nationalist Protesters: 'Some Very Fine People on Both Sides'," Atlantic, August 15, 2017, https://www.theatlantic.com/politics/archive/2017/08/trump-defends-white-nationalist-protesters-some-very-fine-people-on-both-sides/537012/Accessed July 17, 2019.

p. 17, "This is a time to lay…" Ayesha Rascoe, "A Year After Charlottesville, Not Much Has Changed For Trump," NPR, August 11, 2018, https://www.npr.org/2018/08/11/637665414/a-year-after-charlottesville-not-much-has-changed-for-trump Accessed July 17, 2019.

p. 24, "Muslims should die…" Shane Dixon Kavanaugh, "Muslim teen targeted before MAX train slaying: 'Our faces were a trigger'," The Oregonian, August 15, 2018, https://www.oregonlive.com/portland/2018/08/muslim_teen_targeted_before_ma.html Accessed July 17, 2019.

p. 24, "Everywhere I go…" Ibid., Accessed July 17, 2019.

p. 24, "When I see someone…" Chandelis R. Duster, "Charlottesville survivor Marcus Martin still healing after deadly rally," NBC News, December 12, 2017, https://www.nbcnews.com/news/nbcblk/charlottesville-survivor-marcus-martin-still-healing-after-deadly-rally-n828466 Accessed July 17, 2019.

p. 26, "Anyone who needs help…" "Orlando mass shooting is LGBT community's "biggest fear," CBS News, June 12, 2016, https://www.cbsnews.com/news/orlando-nightclub-shooting-lgbt-communitys-biggest-fear/ Accessed July 17, 2019.

p. 26, "It's a message that…" Mary Emily O'Hara, "Wave of Vandalism, Violence Hits LGBTQ Centers Across Nation," NBC News, March 13, 2017, https://www.nbcnews.com/feature/nbc-out/wave-vandalism-violence-hits-lgbtq-centers-across-nation-n732761 Accessed July 17, 2019.

p. 28, "this crazy idea…" Andrew Knapp, "'Hate won't win.' Accused Charleston church shooter faces survivors, families," The Post and Courier, June 18, 2015, https://www.postandcourier.com/archives/hate-won-t-win-accused-charleston-

church-shooter-faces-survivors/article_
f31b2340-902e-5c71-aa5d-8c1fe870a4b2.html
Accessed July 17, 2019.

p. 29, "As a community I..." Debbie Elliot,
"'Unite The Right' Rally Forced Charlottesville To Rethink Town's Racial History," NPR, August 9, 2018, https://www.npr.
org/2018/08/09/637230082/unite-the-right-
rally-forced-charlottesville-to-rethink-town-s-
racial-history Accessed July 17, 2019.

p. 29, "Everything that's been going..." Ibid.,
Accessed July 17, 2019.

p. 30, "I can't see a human..." Audra D.S. Burch,
"In Texas, a Decades-Old Hate Crime, Forgiven
but Never Forgotten," The New York Times, July
9, 2018, https://www.nytimes.com/2018/07/09/
us/james-byrd-jasper-texas-killing.html
Accessed July 17, 2019.

p. 31, "They killed him because..." Ibid.,
Accessed July 17, 2019.

p. 31, "Full of hatred..." Jude Sheerin, "Matthew
Shepard: The murder that changed America,"
BBC News, October 26, 2018, https://www.bbc.
com/news/world-us-canada-45968606 Accessed
July 17, 2019.

p. 34, "Strengthen the protections..." Jeff Zeleny,
"Obama Signs Hate Crime Bill," The New York
Times, October 28, 2009, https://thecaucus.
blogs.nytimes.com/2009/10/28/obama-signs-
hate-crimes-bill/Accessed July 17, 2019.

p. 37, "TV usually depicts killers..." Margaret
Talbot, "The Story of a Hate Crime: What led to
the murder of three Muslim students in Chapel
Hill?" The New Yorker, June 15, 2015, https://
www.newyorker.com/magazine/2015/06/22/
the-story-of-a-hate-crime Accessed July 17,
2019.

p. 41, "Without accurate reporting..." Liz Spikol,
"FBI: Hate Crimes on the Rise," Washington Jewish Week, November 20, 2018, https://washing-
tonjewishweek.com/49670/fbi-hate-crimes-on-
the-rise/featured-left/ Accessed July 17, 2019.

p. 46, "public hanging..." Jane C. Timm, "Police
investigating nooses hung at Mississippi Capitol
to protest state's racial history ahead of Hyde-
Smith vs. Espy runoff," NBC News, November
26, 2018, https://www.nbcnews.com/politics/
elections/nooses-found-hanging-mississippi-
capitol-n940176 Accessed July 17, 2019.

p. 47, "Hail Trump..." Daniel Lombroso and Yoni
Appelbaum, "'Hail Trump!': White Nationalists Salute the President-Elect," The Atlantic,

November 26, 2016, https://www.theatlantic.
com/politics/archive/2016/11/richard-spencer-
speech-npi/508379/ Accessed July 17, 2019.

p. 48, "a response to the..." Richard Perez-Pena
and Megan Specia, "World Reacts to El Paso
Shooting and the Hate That Fueled It," The
New York Times, August 6, 2019, https://www.
nytimes.com/2019/08/06/world/europe/mass-
shooting-international-reaction.html Accessed
August 8, 2019.

p. 48, "We're seeing an unmistakable..." Masood
Farivar, "Hate Crimes in Major US Cities Rise for
Fifth Year in a Row, Data Show," Voice of America, January 31, 2019, https://www.voanews.com/
usa/hate-crimes-major-us-cities-rise-fifth-year-
row-data-show Accessed July 17, 2019.

p. 48, "We are Americans..." Grace Panetta,
"'How hard can that be, to say that Nazis are
bad?': Obama slams Trump's response to violent
protests in Charlottesville," Business Insider,
September 7, 2018, https://www.businessinsid-
er.com/obama-trump-charlottesville-neo-nazis-
speech-illinois-2018-9 Accessed July 17, 2019.

p. 49, "Mr. McKinney, I am..." Michael Janofsky,
"Parents of Gay Obtain Mercy For His Killer,"
The New York Times, November 5, 1999, https://
www.nytimes.com/1999/11/05/us/parents-of-
gay-obtain-mercy-for-his-killer.html Accessed
July 17, 2019.

p. 49, "We wanted the system..." David Crary,
"Views are mixed on hate crime law named
for Matthew Shepard," AP News, October 12,
2018, https://www.apnews.com/a6d811ece-
9254facbc68df40d20e931a Accessed July 17,
2019.

p. 50, "By sharing what you..." Communities
Against Hate, https://communitiesagainsthate.
org/about Accessed July 17, 2019.

p. 54, "We should not kid..." Rachel Hatzipanagos, "How online hate turns into real violence," The Washington Post, November 30,
2018, https://www.washingtonpost.com/
nation/2018/11/30/how-online-hate-speech-
is-fueling-real-life-violence/?utm_term=.
ef919333c8df Accessed July 17, 2019.

p. 56, "I can't believe I..." Richard Fausset,
"Rally by White Nationalists Was Over Almost
Before It Began," The New York Times, August
12, 2018, https://www.nytimes.com/2018/08/12/
us/politics/charlottesville-va-protest-unite-the-
right.html Accessed July 17, 2019.

SELECT BIBLIOGRAPHY

Books

Sethi, Arjun Singh. *American Hate: Survivors Speak Out*. New York: The New Press, 2018.

Websites and Articles

Bryan, Zyahna, "One Year Since Charlottesville: How the City Has Reckoned with Its White Supremacist, Racist History," *Teen Vogue*, August 7, 2018, https://www.teen-vogue.com/story/one-year-since-charlottesville-op-ed-white-supremacist-racist-history Accessed May 6, 2019.

Burch, Audra D. S., "In Texas, a Decades-Old Hate Crime, Forgiven but Never Forgotten," *The New York Times*, July 9, 2018, https://www.nytimes.com/2018/07/09/us/james-byrd-jasper-texas-killing.html Accessed May 6, 2019.

Burke, Daniel, "The Four Reasons People Commit Hate Crimes," CNN, June 12, 2017, https://www.cnn.com/2017/06/02/us/who-commits-hate-crimes/index.html Accessed May 6, 2019.

Dashow, Jordan, "New FBI Statistics Show Alarming Increase in Number of Reported Hate Crimes," Human Rights Campaign, November 13, 2018, https://www.hrc.org/blog/new-fbi-statistics-show-alarming-increase-in-number-of-reported-hate-crimes Accessed May 6, 2019.

DeAngelis, Tori, "Understanding and preventing hate crimes," American Psychological Association, November 2001, https://www.apa.org/monitor/nov01/hatecrimes Accessed May 6, 2019.

Fausset, Richard, "Rally by White Nationalists Was Over Almost Before It Began," *The New York Times*, August 12, 2018, https://www.nytimes.com/2018/08/12/us/politics/charlottesville-va-protest-unite-the-right.html Accessed May 6, 2019.

Freilich, Joshua D., and Steven M. Chermak, "Hate Crimes," The Center for Problem-Oriented Policing, Arizona State University, https://popcenter.asu.edu/content/center-problem-oriented-policing-problem-guides-hate-crimes Accessed May 6, 2019.

Greenblatt, Jonathan, and Elisa Massimino, "Global Crises Are Overshadowing Hate Crimes," *Time*, May 15, 2017, http://time.com/4318817/hate-crimes/ Accessed May 6, 2019.

"Hate Crime Statistics 2017," FBI UCR, U.S. Department of Justice, 2017, https://ucr.fbi.gov/hate-crime/2017/topic-pages/victims Accessed May 6, 2019.

"Hate Crimes Timeline," Human Rights Campaign, https://www.hrc.org/resources/hate-crimes-timeline Accessed May 6, 2019.

Hatzipanagos, Rachel, "How Online Hate Turns into Real-Life Violence," *The Washington Post*, November 30, 2018, https://www.washingtonpost.com/nation/2018/11/30/how-online-hate-speech-is-fueling-real-life-violence/?utm_term=.2a50ca9e07dc Accessed May 6, 2019.

Hauser, Christine, "Matthew Shepard Laid to Rest at National Cathedral Decades After His Murder," *The New York Times*, October 26, 2018, https://www.nytimes.com/2018/10/26/us/matthew-shepard-burial-national-cathedral.html Accessed May 6, 2019.

Hendrix, Steve, "'It's still hard to look at': The Story Behind the Searing Photo of Charlottesville's worst day," *The Washington Post*, August 10, 2018, https://www.washingtonpost.com/graphics/2018/local/charlottesville-photographer-pulitzer-prize-photo/ Accessed May 6, 2019.

Hersher, Rebecca, "'What Happened To You, Dylann?' Victim's Friend Asks Roof At Sentencing," NPR, January 11, 2017, https://www.npr.org/sections/thetwo-way/2017/01/11/509299574/what-happened-to-you-dylann-victims-friend-asks-roof-at-sentencing Accessed May 6, 2019.

McCoy, Terrence, "'Saviors of the white race': Perpetrators of hate crimes see themselves as heroes, researchers say," *The Washington Post*, October 31, 2018, https://www.washingtonpost.com/local/social-issues/saviors-of-the-white-race-perpetrators-of-hate-crimes-see-themselves-as-heroes-researchers-say/2018/10/31/277a2bdc-daeb-11e8-85df-7a6b4d25cfbb_story.html?utm_term=.8f998817de5c Accessed May 6, 2019.

"Post-Charlottesville Hate Crimes Summit Coalition Recommendations to the Department of Justice," The Leadership Conference of Civil & Human Rights, September 15, 2017, https://civilrights.org/resource/post-charlottesville-hate-crime-summit-coalition-recommendations-department-justice/ Accessed May 6, 2019.

Shanmugasundaram, Swathi, "Hate Crimes, Explained," Southern Poverty Law Center, April 15, 2018, https://www.splcenter.org/20180415/hate-crimes-explained Accessed May 6, 2019.

"Ten Ways to Fight Hate: A Community Response Guide," Southern Poverty Law Center, August 14, 2017, https://www.splcenter.org/20170814/ten-ways-fight-hate-community-response-guide Accessed May 6, 2019.

"What we investigate," FBI, https://www.fbi.gov/investigate/civil-rights/hate-crimes Accessed May 6, 2019.

Zelizer, Julian, "Trump Needs to Demilitarize His Rhetoric," *The Atlantic*, October 29, 2018, https://www.theatlantic.com/ideas/archive/2018/10/americas-long-history-anti-semitism/574234/ Accessed May 6, 2019.

About the Author

Danielle Smith-Llera taught children to think and write about literature in the classroom before turning to write books for them. She is the author of scores of children's books, including *Immigration in America: Asylum, Borders, and Conflicts* in this year's set.

INDEX